D0852724

OPEN YOUR
MIND,

OPEN YOUR
LIFE

Open Your Mind, Open Your Life

A LITTLE BOOK OF EASTERN WISDOM

TARO GOLD

**Andrews McMeel
Publishing**

Kansas City

Open Your Mind, Open Your Life:
A Little Book of Eastern Wisdom

For information, write
Andrews McMeel Publishing, LLC,
an Andrews McMeel Universal company,
4520 Main Street,
Kansas City, Missouri 64111.

ISBN-13: 978-0-7407-1446-7
ISBN-10: 0-7407-1446-5

Library of Congress Catalog Card Number:
00-106920

Book design by Holly Camerlinck
Illustrations by Matthew Taylor

With deepest
appreciation to
Dr. Daisaku Ikeda
for showing me
how to live
an open life

■

THOUGHT CREATES REALITY . . .

Everything humanity has ever created began with a thought. The place where you live, the clothes that you wear, and the paper on which these words are written were once only thoughts in someone's mind. Your decision to read this, too, began with a thought.

HAPPINESS SHAPES THOUGHT . . .

Everything we think is colored by our happiness, or lack thereof. Although individual definitions of happiness vary greatly, we all want to be happy. Early in life, we look for happiness among family, friends, even toys. Later in life, we may look for happiness in religion, money, sex, alcohol, education, marriage. . . . We all know where we have looked. But did we find what we were searching for?

OPENNESS MANIFESTS HAPPINESS . . .

Genuine happiness, or enlightenment, is already within us; we have only to reveal it. As spring water rushes through open earth, so happiness flows through open lives. The question is how to open our lives to this inherent joy. The following pages hold answers to that question, thought by thought, from an Eastern perspective. Most of them may be new to you, some may seem like common sense (which is *not* so common), and others are universal truths not unique to the East. May each of them promote lasting happiness and ways of thinking that truly open your life.

*N*ever seek happiness
outside yourself.

■

*L*ife isn't about what happens to us;
it's about how we *perceive*
what happens to us.

■

*M*aster your past in the present,
or the past will master your future.

Focus on the positive in your life,
for what you focus on increases.

■

The pursuit of truth attracts critics.

■

Everything you need
to break unhealthy cycles of behavior
is within you.

■

Refuse to lower yourself to the level
of your antagonist.

*T*he choices we make in thought,
word, and deed inevitably return to us
in kind.

■

*T*hose who have not asked the question
are not ready to accept the answer.

■

*R*emove the internal,
emotional hooks that attract you
to painful situations.

Never let life's hardships
disturb you. After all, no one
can avoid problems,
not even saints or sages.

— NICHIREN

Let go of anger—it is an acid
that burns away the delicate layers
of your happiness.

■

Maintain your composure
under any circumstance.

■

Live in a way that leaves no regrets.

■

Seek to understand your mistakes
so that you may never repeat them.

*E*verything people say or do
is ultimately rooted in the belief that
those actions will lead them to happiness.

■

*T*he person who confesses ignorance
shows it once; the person who conceals it
shows it many times.

—*Japanese proverb*

■

*D*o something today to improve
someone else's life.

The wisest among us often have
the least to say.

■

The lotus flower blooms most beautifully
from the deepest and thickest mud.

■

Looking for lasting happiness outside
yourself is meaningless. It is like
expecting to become fit by watching
other people exercise.

*L*et go of your attachment
to the outcome.

■

*I*f you want one year of prosperity,
plant corn. If you want ten years of
prosperity, grow trees. If you want
one hundred years of prosperity,
educate people.

—*Chinese proverb*

■

*E*mpower yourself.

*I*t is easy to be the person you
have always been, for it requires no change,
no self-reflection, and no growth. It may
appear that changing yourself requires
giving up something. In reality, there is
no need to give up anything—you must
simply add to what has been.

■

*A*lthough the flames of jealousy
are directed toward others, it is the
jealous person who is consumed
by the fire.

*T*he more enlightening a teaching,
the more difficult it is to believe
and even more difficult to practice.

■

*A*n appreciative heart attracts more
of what it appreciates.

■

*R*ather than defeat your enemies,
seek to transform them into allies.

*D*evelop a profound belief in the
universal law of cause and effect—the
empowering conviction that we all
ultimately direct our own lives.

■

*J*ust as we cannot see our own faces
without looking into a mirror, we cannot
know ourselves without looking
at our relationships.

■

*F*lowing water never goes bad.

—*Chinese proverb*

*O*ur past and our future simultaneously
exist in our present.

◾

*N*onviolence is the greatest virtue,
cowardice the greatest vice—nonviolence
springs from love, cowardice from hate.
—*Mahatma Gandhi*

◾

*T*ruth has the power to dispel the
darkness of ignorance—just as a candle
has the power to light a cave that has
been dark for a million years.

Your actions are simultaneously the result of past karma and the creation of new karma. Action creates memory, and memory creates desire. Desire produces further action, which continues the cycle of karma. To be aware of this reality and to master your actions are the keys to creating the karma of happiness.

■

A great mentor is one who aims for others' abilities to surpass his own.

*I*n thinking, keep to the simple.
In conflict, be fair and generous.
In governing, don't try to control.
In work, do what you enjoy.
In family life, be completely present.

—*Lao Tzu*

■

*F*ame, material wealth, and social status
do not guarantee happiness; in fact,
they often hinder it.

$\mathcal{T}$o a great extent, the people with whom you choose to associate influence the direction of your life.

■

$\mathcal{W}$hen you cannot lift something, you might think it is too heavy—but perhaps it is you who are too weak.

■

$\mathcal{F}$all seven times, stand up eight.

—*Japanese proverb*

*S*trive most to understand
what you fear most.

■

*K*nowledge comes from without—
wisdom comes from within.

■

*W*hat would your current frustrations
look like from the vantage point
of the final days of your life?

*E*nlightenment, or true happiness, is not a transcendental state. It is a condition of broad wisdom, boundless energy, and good fortune wherein we each shape our own destiny, find fulfillment in daily activities, and come to understand our ultimate purpose in life.

—*Josei Toda*

■

*A*ccept praise and believe it as readily as you would criticism.

$\mathcal{Y}$ou are what you believe.

■

$\mathcal{W}$hen the student is ready,
the teacher will appear.

—*Buddhist proverb*

■

$\mathcal{W}$e think and behave within the
boundaries of our beliefs. The key, then,
to fulfilling our potential without
limitations is to master our beliefs,
to master our minds.

The idea that life and death are separate is
the reasoning of dreams, deluded and
inverted. If when wide awake we examine
our true nature, we will find no beginning
that requires our being born and no end
that requires our dying. What we will find
is the essence of life, which cannot be
burned by apocalyptic flames or worn away
by flood or cut down by sword or pierced
by arrow. It is not too large to enter the seed
of a flower without the seed expanding.
It is not too small to fill the entire universe
without the universe contracting.

—*Nichiren*

*H*ave no fear of evil people.
What you should beware are evil friends.
Why? Because evil people can destroy only
your body, they cannot destroy your mind.
An evil friend can destroy both.

■

*M*any times the best way to fight
is not to fight at all.

■

*E*verything abides by the law
of cause and effect.

*R*emember your debts of gratitude.

■

*L*ife appears throughout the universe
wherever and whenever conditions are
right, much as waves appear in the ocean
when windy conditions arise. As a wave
is simply an individual expression of the
greater ocean, so too are we expressions
of the greater life of the universe.

■

*B*e concerned more with how you live
than with how long.

When you encounter someone
greater than yourself, turn your
thoughts to becoming his equal.
When you encounter someone
lesser than you, look within
and examine your own self.

— CONFUCIUS

To change our lives, we must first
change our minds.

■

People have been deluded into believing
that the key to happiness lies in
reforming their exterior. In fact, it is
one's interior that holds the key.

■

Become a master of words.

■

You can make the place you are now
your paradise.

*L*et go of
whatever holds you back.

∎

A person writing at night may put out
the lamp, but the words he has written
will remain. It is the same with the destiny
we create for ourselves in this world.

—*Shakyamuni*

∎

*T*here is nothing more precious
than life itself.

$\mathcal{A}$ll the answers exist within your actions.

◼

$\mathcal{T}$he true nature of your life exists
everywhere at once across all space
and time—for the nature of your life is
the nature of the universe itself.

◼

$\mathcal{T}$he closer you stand to the lighthouse,
the darker it gets.

—*Japanese proverb*

25

*J*ust as the two sides of a coin are distinct
yet inseparable, our lives have a physical,
tangible dimension and a spiritual,
intangible one. We may differentiate
between body and mind, but at their most
fundamental level, they are inseparable.

■

*M*isfortune comes from one's mouth
and ruins him, but fortune comes
from one's mind and makes him
worthy of respect.

—*Nichiren*

*L*asting goodness works
at the pace of a snail.

■

*T*here has never been, nor will there
ever be, a life free from problems. It is
not the presence of problems but how
we tackle them that determines the
quality of our lives.

■

*Y*our dream is possible.

There are four major factors in achieving goals: (1) *objective*, the goal itself; (2) *you*, the person striving to attain the goal; (3) *actions*, the efforts made to attain the goal; (4) *positioning*, your situation upon achieving the goal. Of these four, you and your objective are the most important factors. For example, if your self-image and your objectives don't match, if you don't believe you are worthy of achieving your goals, you will not achieve them no matter what actions you take. When you believe you deserve to attain your goals, however, even minor actions yield great results.

*The fool who knows he is a fool
is for that very reason wise.
The fool who thinks himself wise
is the greatest fool of all.*

— SHAKYAMUNI

*T*he defining characteristic of true compassion is that the helper and the person helped are equally in need of each other for their personal growth.

■

*O*f all strategies, to know when to quit may be the best.

—*Chinese proverb*

■

*A*ll great masters in any endeavor of life have first had an excellent mentor.

*T*here is nothing we can say or do to change another person. People will change only when they are ready. The only people we have the power to change are ourselves. When we change ourselves, however, we often find that the change we desired in others happens as well.

■

*T*he true mission of religion is to help people manifest the power within themselves to overcome their difficulties and be happy.

Your behavior while people are watching is important. However, your behavior while no one is watching is more important, for it reveals your true character.

■

Develop a broad compassion that reaches beyond your surroundings and extends to unknown places.

■

Strive to learn from noble people.

The universe is life itself. When we die, our lives melt back into the greater life of the universe and are nowhere to be found, much like the interval of sleep when our minds are seemingly nowhere. Just as we resume our mental activities from the previous day upon awakening, so too are we born with our karma from previous existences. In this way, just as we sleep and wake, we are born and die, maintaining an eternal cycle of life.

—*Josei Toda*

He who knows others is wise; he who knows himself is enlightened.

—*Lao Tzu*

◾

No one can give you abilities. For example, an Olympic athlete works with a trainer to develop her abilities, but the trainer only helps manifest what was inherent all along. Likewise, no one can give you happiness. At most, others simply help manifest the joy that was within you from the beginning.

*T*hose who maintain a clear sense
of purpose in life are strengthened
by hardship.

∎

*W*hen a caged bird sings,
birds flying in the sky are thereby
summoned and gather around; and when
the flying birds gather around, the bird
in the cage strives to get out.

—*Nichiren*

*W*isdom, courage, and compassion—
three essential elements of a noble life.

■

*A*lways expect the best, and
be prepared for the worst.

■

*T*o be wronged is nothing
unless you continue to remember it.

—*Confucius*

■

*M*ake time each day for self-reflection.

*L*ive lightly on the Earth.

—*Tsunesaburo Makiguchi*

■

*T*he surest path is one dedicated
to a greater cause.

■

*I*gnorance breeds fear.
Fear breeds hate.
Hate breeds violence.

*T*he mind is a powerful and
mysterious force. It can make the best
of the worst and the worst of the best.

■

*O*utward appearances are unimportant—
your heart is what truly matters.

■

*S*cientific and technological advances
used against the greater good of humanity
reflect a society whose technology has
surpassed its spirituality.

$\mathcal{B}$e an ally to those who are suffering.

■

$\mathcal{E}$ducation breeds confidence.
Confidence breeds hope.
Hope breeds peace.

■

$\mathcal{A}$ truly wise person will not be
carried away by any of the eight winds:
prosperity, decline, disgrace, honor, praise,
censure, suffering, pleasure.

—*Nichiren*

$\mathcal{W}$e can try many ways to get rid of
the darkness, but none is as effective
as simply increasing the light.

■

$\mathcal{Y}$our teacher can open the door, but
you must enter by yourself.

—*Chinese proverb*

■

$\mathcal{A}$ dynamic life is a constant struggle
against complacency.

The Lotus Sutra, the ancient teaching
that asserts all people have enlightenment
within them and are essentially equals,
is a radical teaching. If it were not,
then racial, sexual, and age
discrimination, not to mention violence,
terrorism, and war, would not exist.

■

The higher the position a leader
holds in the political, the religious, or
any realm, the more humble he or she
should become.

41

*I*t is much easier to *say* what is just and
right than to *do* what is just and right.

■

*E*verything, including all people,
exists only through relationships
with other people or things.
Nothing exists in isolation or absolute
independence. No person or thing
can arise of, for, or by its own accord.
Everything is interdependent.

■

*A*lways act upon a generous impulse.

The heart is what matters most. One sutra tells the story of a boy named Doji who had nothing to offer the Buddha but a mud pie. Others offered gold and gems, but their hearts were insincere. Since the Buddha was worthy of great respect and since Doji's heart was sincere, a single mud pie became such a great offering that Doji was later reborn as King Ashoka.

■

There is always a piece of fortune in misfortune.

—*Japanese proverb*

$\mathcal{F}$ocus less on treating the symptom
than on eliminating the cause.

■

$\mathcal{G}$o abroad.

■

$\mathcal{H}$atred never ceases through hatred.
By compassion alone does it cease.

—*Shakyamuni*

■

$\mathcal{Y}$our hopes and dreams are far more
valid than your doubts and fears.

*S*uffering ultimately
arises from delusion.

■

*U*se the power of your imagination
every day.

■

*E*ndeavors accomplished quickly
and easily rarely endure.

■

*J*udge your actions by the
value they create.

*H*umans cannot create matter. We can,
however, create value. Creating value is,
in fact, our very humanity. When we praise
people for their strength of character,
we are actually acknowledging their
ability to create value.

—*Tsunesaburo Makiguchi*

■

*N*o one has the right
to cause others to suffer.

*D*on't confuse the extent of one's fame
with the extent of one's character.

■

*W*e often see others as we see ourselves.
Those caught up in deceit and
posturing tend to mistrust even the
well-meaning actions of others. In contrast, a
person of integrity tends to trust that
others are the same, even when they are not.

■

*S*trive to live unrestricted
by your past experiences.

One who is afraid to examine the past
cannot see the future.

■

In all affairs of life, at every moment,
we have a choice.

■

The birth of an idea in your mind
and the birth of a celestial star in
distant space—both arise from the same
latent field of cosmic energy.

*F*avorable circumstances may be pleasant,
but they rarely strengthen one's character.
The greater the person, the greater the
adversity he or she has overcome.

■

*I*f you befriend another person
but lack the mercy to correct him,
you are in fact his enemy.

—*Chang-an*

■

*A*s long as bias exists, expect justice
to be the exception instead of the rule.

$\mathcal{N}$onviolence requires much more
courage than violence.

—*Mahatma Gandhi*

■

$\mathcal{T}$here are three kinds of law:
social and moral law, or culturally
acceptable behavior; civil and criminal law,
or legally accepted behavior; and universal
law, or cause and effect. We may avoid
the consequences of breaking the first two,
but never the third.

*T*here once was a baby circus elephant who couldn't break free from her leg chain, though she tried and tried. Eventually, she gave up altogether. Years later, she still had that little chain around her leg. Although she was strong enough to break free, in her mind she had long since accepted that she could not. Emotional chains, after all, are the hardest to break.

$\mathcal{N}$ature, in all its functions, is remarkably purposeful. Who, then, could possibly imagine that he or she was born into this world for no purpose?

■

$\mathcal{T}$here may be nothing more treacherous than false knowledge.

■

$\mathcal{A}$s water carves through stone, those who persevere will win.

*W*hen someone's character is not clear
to you, look at that person's friends.

—*Japanese proverb*

■

*B*irth and death, appearance and
disappearance, gain and loss, existence
and extinction—all are essential and
everlasting processes.

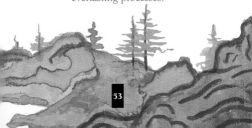

53

*P*eople become what they expect
themselves to become.

—*Mahatma Gandhi*

∎

*O*ur opinions, attitudes, and perceptions
are colored by our memories of past
experiences, which form our biases
and predispositions. Our current
viewpoint, then, is simply a reflection
of our ever-changing memory.

Tz'u-en taught that negative actions arise from one or more of fourteen categories: (1) arrogance; (2) carelessness; (3) arbitrary, egotistical judgment; (4) shallow, self-satisfied understanding; (5) attachment to earthly desires; (6) lack of seeking spirit; (7) failure to believe in cause and effect; (8) antipathy; (9) deluded doubt of the truth; (10) vilification; (11) contempt; (12) hatred; (13) jealousy; (14) grudges.

*W*hat irritates us most about others is
often what we dislike most about ourselves.

■

*E*xamine the events in your life
for patterns.

■

*Y*ou create your memories and
experiences, not the other way around.

■

*D*on't give others what they don't want.

—*Japanese proverb*

Nothing exists entirely alone; everything exists in relation to everything else. Where there is light, there is shadow; where there is birth, there is death; where there is open, there is closed; where there is one, there is other. By the same reasoning, where there is sadness, there is joy; where there is delusion, there is enlightenment.

*T*here once was a woman who lost her child to disease. Crazy with grief, she stumbled through the city begging for medicine to bring her child back. When she came upon the Buddha, he told her he would give her the medicine she needed. He asked her to find a poppy from a house where no one had lost a loved one. In her quest, she found there was not even one such home. She realized that death is a fact of life, and that she was not alone in her grief. In this way, the Buddha awakened her wisdom, restoring peace to her heart.

The process of learning
is often more important
than what is being learned.

■

Change for the better requires effort.
Change for the worse needs none.

■

If that which is within is not right,
it is futile to pray for that which is without.

—*Japanese proverb*

$\mathcal{B}$ecome a revisionist of
your own history. Go back into your
halls of memory and find the courage
to view those experiences again—only
this time through the clear vision of
retrospection. Give yourself the answers
you did not have then, learn what you
once failed to learn, and allow yourself
and others to have been wrong. Then let
it go. When you do this, you will feel
a sense of boundless, joyful freedom.

One who lives life with passion is like a brightly burning fire. A small, dim fire can easily be extinguished by gusts of wind, but a large, bright one will grow bigger as the wind grows stronger. In the same way, the more obstacles a passionate person encounters, the brighter and stronger that person grows.

■

Mistaking subjective values for objective truth leads to no good.

*M*anifest the courage to discard the shallow and seek the profound.

■

*A*ll phenomena, even the most solid rock, are transient.

■

*R*emember that sometimes *not* getting what you want is the best thing for you.

■

*W*ise people never rely upon their memory of past experience alone.

An unhappy person and a happy one will have different perceptions of the same circumstances. The difference lies not in the circumstances but in the two states of life.

■

Guessing is cheap; guessing wrong is expensive.

—*Chinese proverb*

■

Nature makes no mistakes.

*L*et go of hate—people consumed by it
often become exactly what they once hated.

■

*L*isten more than you speak.

■

*T*he worst dilemmas are often the best
opportunities in disguise.

■

*W*hen in debate, remember that you
and the point you are trying to make
are two different things.

Know the difference between instinct
and habit. Trust your instincts—
question your habits.

■

All that is comes from the mind;
it is based on the mind, it is fashioned
by the mind.

—*Shakyamuni*

■

It is better to live one week of integrity
than to live ten years of deceit.

*P*ractice putting your own feelings
and judgments aside when you listen
to others. Try to look at the matter
from their viewpoint.

■

*T*rue words are often not beautiful,
just as beautiful words are often not true.

—*Japanese proverb*

■

*E*njoying the journey is even better
than arriving at the destination.

*T*here are three types of cause: thoughts, words, and deeds. Of the three, thoughts are the most powerful, for words and deeds arise only from thoughts.

■

*U*ntil we learn the lessons inherent in unpleasant experiences, they will continue to hold power over us, and we will feel compelled to repeat them.

■

*R*emember who you knew you were when you were a child.

*W*hen we are upset, it's easy to blame others. However, the true cause of our feelings is within us. For example, imagine yourself as a glass of water. Now, imagine past negative experiences as sediment at the bottom of your glass. Next, think of others as spoons. When one stirs, the sediment clouds your water. It may appear that the spoon caused the water to cloud— but if there were no sediment, the water would remain clear no matter what. The key, then, is to identify our sediment and actively work to remove it.

—*Josei Toda*

A master of one's inner experience
is a master of life.

∎

*S*trive to achieve whatever you think
you cannot, for it is on the path
toward your impossible dream that you
will find what you truly seek.

∎

*A*s spring water rushes through
open earth, so happiness flows
through open lives.

*O*nly *you* can make you happy.

■

*T*reasures of wealth are good.
Treasures of health are better.
Treasures of the heart are best.

■

*I*ntuition transcends the
limitations of reason.

$\mathcal{D}$o what you mean.

◼

$\mathcal{P}$eople naturally fear misfortune and long
for good fortune; but if the distinction is
carefully studied, misfortune often turns
out to be fortune and good fortune to be
misfortune. Wise people are therefore
never unduly elated by apparent fortune
nor unduly upset by apparent misfortune.

◼

$\mathcal{W}$inter always turns to spring.

—$\mathcal{N}$ichiren

*E*ven the greatest strategy is useless
in the hands of a coward.

■

*M*any people embrace honorable
philosophies, preaching them far and wide,
yet live to betray their intent.

■

*B*eware the winds of fame and fortune.
Despite their advantages, left unchecked
they can extinguish the flame of wisdom.

There is a bird that lives deep in the snowy mountains. Tortured by night's numbing cold, it cries that it will build a warm nest in the morning. Yet, when day breaks, it sleeps the day away, basking in the warmth of the sun. So it continues, crying vainly throughout its life. People are often the same, lamenting their circumstances yet passing by every opportunity to change.

■

Be self-reliant.

From the perspective of the ultimate
reality of the universe, there is no
such thing as "mine."

■

Keep a green tree in your heart
and perhaps a songbird will come.

—*Chinese proverb*

■

Dream more of becoming
than of obtaining.

■

Life is as fleeting as the morning dew.

*People of great character
conduct themselves with dignity,
even in times of crisis or despair—
they do not complain, panic,
or lose hope even under
the most difficult circumstances.*

When bandits plague a king, he must find out where their camp is before he can attack them. Likewise, when we are beset by restless passions, we should first ascertain their origins.

■

When we enter a house, we first notice the interior and only later look out the windows. In like manner, our mind's eye cannot correctly see the external before it correctly sees the internal.

Clouds can obscure the moon, but they cannot change it or affect its inherent nature. Likewise, our mind is often clouded by delusions, yet our true mind, our true essence, remains unaffected.

∎

Both water and oil become round in a round glass and square in a square one. Water and oil have no shape in and of themselves. The same is true of good and evil. Good and evil actions may take the same shape, yet the wise can perceive the difference.

$\mathcal{B}$ecome the master of your mind.

■

$\mathcal{N}$ever compromise your dreams.

■

$\mathcal{Y}$ou cannot do right in one department
of life while occupied doing wrong in
any other department. Life is one
indivisible whole.

—*Mahatma Gandhi*

■

$\mathcal{G}$reed arises from an inaccurate
perception of one's true desires.

The fires of human desire burn endlessly.
Trying to extinguish them is like trying
to quench thirst with salt water. Instead of
eliminating desires, we should seek
to transform them.

■

Change on a fundamental level
is rarely easy.

■

People should cherish one another
for their positive traits and help
one another with their negative traits.

From unhealthy desires unhealthy
actions follow; from unhealthy actions
unhappy experiences follow—like an
endlessly rotating wheel, which we
must learn to stop.

■

Some people suffer as much from wealth
as others do from poverty.

■

Do more than expected.

*C*oncealing shortcomings while
boasting virtues defines arrogance.

—*Miao-lo*

■

*F*eelings of defensiveness are rooted
in self-doubt.

■

*M*ost people spend their time longing
for results without undertaking efforts
to achieve them.

Never compare yourself with others.

■

The wise are sensitive to right and wrong;
they cease doing anything as soon as
they see that it is wrong, and they
appreciate those who call their
attention to it.

■

The biggest room in the world is the
room for improvement.

—Japanese proverb

$\mathcal{A}$ man found a long stretch of beach upon which hundreds of starfish had been stranded by a great storm. He observed a boy cupping the starfish in his hands one by one and gently placing them back into the sea. The man asked the boy: "What does it matter? You'll never save them all." The boy smiled. "It matters to the ones I save."

■

$\mathcal{G}$reat good is often born of one small act of kindness.

*I*nconspicuous, spiritual treasures
such as self-respect, hope, wisdom, and
compassion are the greatest fortune;
without these, conspicuous wealth is
trifling at best.

■

*I*t is easy to shield our bodies against
poisoned arrows from without
but difficult to shield our minds against
poisoned darts from within.

—*Shakyamuni*

*A*pparent distinctions among things exist
only in our minds. For example, in the
sky there is no distinction of east and west.
People create such distinctions and then
believe them to be true. We do the same
in everyday life—making distinctions,
such as "us" and "them," where none exist
and then believe them to be real.

■

*T*he means by which an end
is reached must exemplify the value
of the end itself.

*To teach another something
is like oiling the wheels of a heavy cart
so that they will turn.*

— NICHIREN